How to Stay

GW01086535

7 Easy Steps to Master Self Motivation, Gamification, Willpower, Work Life Balance & Motivate Yourself

Miles Toole

More by Miles Toole

Discover all books from the Personal Productivity Series by Miles Toole at:

bit.ly/miles-toole

Book 1: *How to Be Productive*

Book 2: *How to Manage Time*

Book 3: *How to Be Organized*

Book 4: *How to Stay Focused*

Book 5: *How to Set Goals*

Book 6: *How to Stop Procrastinating*

Book 7: *How to Change Habits*

Book 8: *How to Stay Motivated*

Themed book bundles available at discounted prices:

bit.ly/miles-toole

Copyright

Table of Contents

Introduction

Welcome to *"How to Stay Motivated"*. You could be a happy person in general whose energetic and motivated. But every now and then, everyone falls into a rut. You're not alone if you find yourself experience the occasional moments where you feel listless and demotivated. You feel burned out, and you've lost some of that fiery passion you initially started out as you worked toward your goals. You don't feel like doing anything. Now, some people can recover fairly quickly, while others need a little bit of a push. You see, there is a difference between a temporary rut and *depression.* The thing about demotivation and depression is that the two could almost be mistaken for each other because they may appear almost alike. But if you look just a little bit closer, you'll find that the two are very different in terms of states of being. If you do believe that what you're experiencing is depression, the strategies in this guide might help you gradually work your way out of it too, but if you do need more help, it's okay to talk to somebody about the struggles you're going through.

No matter what goal you've set for yourself, sticking to your goal and seeing it through to the end is not an easy task. Even some of the most successful people you see out there today have struggled to stay on track at times. There's a reason people find it hard to stick to the resolutions they set every New Year's Eve. Why is it so hard to stick to what we were determined to do not too long ago? *Motivation.* Motivation is the strongest factor needed to sustained change to happen. The problem with motivation is that it tends to fluctuate, even worse when we have to do an activity we're dreading or not interested in. The challenging moments that we face as we're working toward our goal or when we're pushed out of our comfort zone are the times when we need motivation and willpower more than ever.

Motivation is the reason behind your decisions and your actions. It is the driving force behind your willingness to go the distance to achieve your goals. It is the reason you stand up again and keep pushing forward no matter how many times you get knocked down in life by the obstacles you face. Your motivation is the force that pushes you to do something. It is an internal phenomenon, and everyone has it within them to boost their motivation with the right strategies and techniques. Which is exactly what motivated you to go through this guide today. Your desire for positive change in your life has fueled you to reach this point. The next few chapters are going to guide you through the steps you need to take to fan the flames of your motivation so that even if it does die out every now and then, you know exactly what you need to do to get that fire burning again. Let's get right into it.

Chapter 1: Step 1 – Break Bad Morning Routines

Let's talk about your morning routine. The internet has no shortage of advice when it comes to morning routines from blogs to books and podcast episodes, but there is a problem with all of the information circulating, and it is important to be aware of it. It seems like most of the content is geared toward focusing on *what you need to add to your morning routine* instead of what you should do to break out of your bad morning routine habits. This Chapter is going to take a different approach by focusing on what you should *stop doing*. In doing so, you'll hopefully be able to stay motivated and increase your willpower for success.

What Exactly Is a Bad Habit?

In Charles Duhigg's book, *The Power of Habit*, he defines a habit in general as an ingrained pattern of behavior that has three stages:

- The cue (what triggers your behavior)
- The action (the action you take from that cue)
- The reward

He also mentioned that once a habit becomes truly, deeply rooted and ingrained, and you've gone through it several times, a fourth component comes into the equation, and that's *craving*. When the cue is triggered in your mind, there is an intense craving for that reward. It's important to understand this every habit has a reward; otherwise, you wouldn't do it. So essentially, a bad habit is really any habit that stands in opposition to your long-term goals, be it living a healthy life, or maintaining good relationships, achieving better work-life balance, or staying motivated and determined.

How to Break Your Bad Morning Routine Habits

Success is not about luck. It's about *routine.* It's about the little things that you do each day that lead you one step closer to success. The idea that it is crucial to begin the day as efficiently as possible is not a new concept. It is something that has been touted time and time again. These claims are everywhere you look, from the advice given to you by others to the numerous online articles and books you'll find about why it is so important to establish a routine for yourself, and the best way to start creating a morning routine that is both powerful and effective for yourself is by breaking the following, common bad morning habits:

Quit the Complaining

You'd be surprised at how much complaining you could be guilty of each day once you start paying attention. Complaining kills willpower and motivation. A lot of people wake up in the morning, and what's the first thing they do? *Complain. Be negative.* They complain about waking up so early in the morning. They complain about going to a job they hate and how horrible the commute is. They complain about being tired. The problem is that words have a tangible effect on your mindset. Your choice of words and the way you express them has a tangible effect on your motivation because it is impacting your mindset. It's going to be impossible to start the day on a positive note if the very first thing you do in the morning is set the tone by being negative.

Quit Checking Your Phone

The second item on the list has to do with none other than your *phone.* Yes, that magical little rectangle that is permanently found in your hands or in your pocket. That little piece of plastic that has us all hooked for hours. Stop checking your phone the first thing in the morning. There are two good reasons to break out of this bad habit. For one thing, if social media is your first task of the day as soon as you wake up, you're giving in to the craving that we all have but won't admit. The craving for *novelty* and is going to counteract everything you've been working so hard to do to build that focus and concentration. Instead, if you waited a little longer before you picked up your phone and checked your notifications, you're teaching your brain discipline and the art of resisting temptation. You're teaching your brain that the novelty of checking your social media feeds does not control you. The second reason to stop checking your phone in the morning while you're in bed is that you end up wasting time. Too much time, in fact. Maybe you tell yourself you're only going to check it for 5-minutes. The next thing you know, 30-minutes have gone by. This is valuable time that could be spent doing something a lot more productive. Plus, it's not healthy to scroll through your phone in bed. You're either propped on one elbow or lying on your back with your phone held above you. Either way, you're putting unnecessary pressure on certain joints and nerves when you do that, and you may not be feeling the impact now, but you will later.

Quit Starting the Day with Negative News

This bad habit is also linked to starting the morning complaining and checking your social media feed. Not everything you see online is going to be positive. In fact, there's more negativity out there today than ever before, and we're more exposed to it now because we're so connected to our mobile devices. Just like complaining first thing in the morning, this sets the tone for a negative day and mindset ahead when the first thing you see is negative stories and bad news. You'll be down the rabbit hole of negativity before you know it and you're once again wasting time in the process. Read an inspirational book, or tailor your newsfeed in such a way that you're receiving more positive news first. Another option is to check your newsfeed much, much later in the day if this is something you really have to do.

Quit the Unhealthy Breakfast Cycle

You need a lot of energy throughout the day to stay motivated and keep your willpower strong to avoid giving in to temptation. Eating an unhealthy breakfast full of carbs and sugar is a bad habit. One you've probably been indulging in for years without giving it a second thought. Sugars and carbs are not going to sustain your energy throughout the rest of the day. Unfortunately, the bad breakfast habit is one that is easy to fall prey to, especially when you're in a rush out the door in the morning to get to work. To break this habit, one approach would be to meal prep. Cook a week's worth of meals in advance, so you don't need to spend any extra time prepping and preparing your food. Keep them in the fridge, heat them up, and go when it's time to eat. This includes breakfast too.

Quit the Snooze-Button Addiction

Each time you hit the snooze button; you're making the first act of your day a *failed act.* You're admitting that you've already been defeated and the day has not even started yet. How? Because the night before, you set a goal to wake up at a certain time and you failed to do this because you hit the snooze button. Once the alarm rings, it is impossible to carry on with the quality sleep you were enjoying before anyway, so why not spring out of bed with the discipline and determination you and the night before? You set the alarm for a reason, after all. Might as well stick to it and make that a daily exercise in building your discipline muscle.

Quit the Messy Workspace

A messy and cluttered environment is an unproductive one. Would you feel productive if you saw your workspace in a mess the next morning? Probably not. A messy environment might not seem like a big deal, but it bothers you a lot more than you know. The evidence is in the lack of motivation you feel when you sit down and try to get your work done but struggle throughout the day. A good habit to start developing to break the unproductive cycle would be to leave your workspace exactly as you found it once you're done with it. Tidying up might feel like it requires a bit more time and effort, but it balances out when you save yourself time from having to do it the next day, and you can get right down to work. A tidy-up routine is a good routine to start implementing.

Quit the Irregular Sleep Patterns

Getting quality sleep at night sets you up for the energy that you need the next day to stay motivated. An inconsistent sleep routine has a negative impact on your body. Your body and your mind need quality sleep at night and enough hours to rest and recharge after the busy day you've had. If you deprive your body of this crucial recharge time, you're going to struggle to maintain your energy levels the next morning. Compare that to the days when you've had a good night's sleep and think about how well-rested you feel on those days. How much more enthusiasm and energy you have when you wake up in the morning. All because your body had a good night's sleep and the rest it needed. When your energy is compromised, so is your productivity. The best thing you can do in your quest to develop greater levels of motivation is to establish a wake-sleep routine that and time that is consistent.

Chapter 2: Step 2 – Stop Wasting Time

Time. It's something that seems to constantly slip through our fingers. How often have you felt that you never have enough time in a day to complete the things you want to do? How many times have you wished you had more time? Time feels like it is slipping through our fingers because all of us have a tendency to waste more time than we should. We've all been there. Those little tiny bouts of guilt you feel over how much time you wasted scrolling through Netflix, or how many hours you spent on the couch during the weekend binging your favorite show because it was too good to stop.

Of course, it needs to be mentioned that we are just as guilty of wasting time on things that don't induce as much guilt because they don't appear to be timewasters. Taking on too many commitments, for example, is one way that you're wasting time if those commitments are not actively contributing toward bettering your life or one step closer to your goals. When you're stretched too thin, you're stressed out and you end up having to take more time-outs than you normally would, which in a way is also a waste of time. Taking time to recharge every now and then is good, but when it happens too frequently, it's going to impede the speed at which you can accomplish your tasks anyway.

Why Do We Waste So Much Precious Time?

You will subconsciously emulate the company that you keep, and if you're constantly surrounded by people who are consistently unproductive and time-wasters, or if you grew up around family members who weren't as productive as they should be, you may be prone to falling into the time-wasting pattern more than you realize. Living in a world today that is designed for convenience certainly isn't helping matters. In fact, our lifestyle choices could be feeding into our time-wasting tendencies. One example of this phenomenon is none other than social media apps. You've got your digital devices, Netflix, cable, Hulu, comfortable homes, sofas that make us not want to leave it for hours on end, or even friends and family who may be love to chat for hours on end that distract you from the tasks you're supposed to do. All of these options are certainly far more appealing than getting work done, and it can be difficult to motivate yourself to do something productive, especially when we feel such a strong desire to just give in and succumb to temptation because it feels a whole lot better than working.

The truth is if you're not disciplined enough to put in the work and the effort, you're never going to accomplish the results that you want. It is as simple as that. Procrastinating and wasting time is easy. Anyone could waste time with a snap of a finger. All you need to do is pick up your phone, open any social media app, and the next thing you know, an hour has gone by, and nothing is accomplished. Being hardworking and motivated to reach goals is the one that is difficult because it requires willpower, self-motivation, and discipline, three qualities that you need to have about you if you hope to achieve success. No self-discipline and motivation will prove to be a hindrance, because the level of success you achieve is going to boil down to your attitude at the end of the day. If you spend most of your time just wasting time, then expect that the results you are going to get are going to be along those lines.

How to Stop Wasting Time

Managing your time better is not as difficult to begin as you may think. It starts by sitting down and taking a long, hard look at how you are currently spending your time. Evaluate it with honesty, because only then will you be able to see where improvement needs to be made. Evaluate how you spend the time that you have right now. For example, if you commute to work, how do you spend on time onboard public transport until you arrive at your destination? Finding the little areas in your life, which could be maximized to include tasks that you need to do during the day is how you maximize your time. If you had a task to listen to an audiobook, for instance, why not do that during your back and forth commute from work? Once you've done an assessment of your current routine and habits, it's time to implement these effective measures that will help you stop wasting time:

Use A Time-Tracking Tool

There are a lot of apps these days that help you track your time and how you're using it. One such app is Toggle, a manual time-tracking app that allows you to key in how much time you spend on each task you undertake throughout the day. Why consider giving Toggle a try? For one thing, tracking your time manually forces you to pay attention to exactly what you're doing and how much time you spend doing it. Automatic time-tracking apps are not going to be as efficient, because, without the act of manually logging your hours, it's still possible to spend too much time on a task and not realize it. Manually tracking allows you to accurately see how well you're spending your time on a daily basis, and you can then make the necessary changes you need going forward so you're spending that time more efficiently.

Be Clear About Your Priorities

Once you have established the clear goals of each task, and the priority that each task should take, it is now time to carry out those tasks based on the order of priority. Be clear about this and write it down on a piece of paper if it helps you see it clearer. Without being clear on your priorities and what they represent on your schedule, it can be easy to take on far too many commitments and become "unnecessarily busy." Having your priorities clearly defined will help you decide if a new commitment is worth it or not.

Design A Productive Environment

Is your current environment conducive to boosting your productivity? Or is it filled with distractions that keep shifting your focus away from the tasks you're meant to be concentrating on? The right environment is every bit as important as anything else when it comes to time management, and continuous distraction will only lead you away from achieving your goals on time. If you've been finding it difficult previously to manage your tasks effectively, this could be why and perhaps it is time for an assessment of your current environment to see what elements need to be changed and removed.

Do Something About Your Distractions

Did you know that you lose more time than you think when you're distracted? Even if it is just for a minute or two because all those minutes add up. Phone calls, chats, texts, quick chats with colleagues, several coffee breaks in a day, all those add up and you suddenly realize that you've lost more time than you should in a day getting nothing done. If you want to be in control and the master of your own time, it starts with eliminating all the distractions you currently have around you. Remove anything that might even be potentially distracting from your workspace, keep your phone on silent when you're working on. Commit to not letting any distractions take your attention away from what you're supposed to be doing. Take a break after you've completed a task, but avoid being distracted before.

Grouping Your Tasks

Group similar tasks together so you can work on it in one-go and knock them off your list quicker. This saves you a lot of time when you can work on similar or related tasks so you don't run the risk of wasting too much time having to go back and forth or doing repetitive work. Avoid multitasking, because this can be counterproductive towards maximizing your time efficiently. You need to keep your mind sharp and focused on just one task at a time before moving onto another; you will find it much better to yield results this way. A lot of the time, you are stressed because you're trying to think about and manage too many things at once, so shift your mindset and focus on just one task at a time.

Saying No and Being Okay with It

This is a major one and probably the one on the list that is the hardest for most people to do. Saying "no" can often induce a lot of feelings of guilt, especially when you're a people-pleaser, and you can't stand the thought that someone might be mad or upset with you because you said "no." Saying "no" is an integral time-management skill if you want to put a stop to being perpetually overcommitted. You have to learn to say "no" if you want to prioritize the things that matter and achieve better work-life balance when your schedule is not filled up unnecessarily. Saying "no" can make it feel like you're letting an opportunity slip through your fingers, but remember that every time you say "yes" to one thing, you're saying "no" to something else. If that "yes" is not something that is aligned with your current priorities or goals, then you're better off saying "no" and wait for the next opportunity to come by.

Chapter 3: Step 3 – Adopt the Habits That Organized People Live By

There are two ways you could do something. You could do it right the first time, or you could do it *again.* That's a pretty powerful statement to think about, especially after the previous Chapter that talks about not wasting time any more than you should be doing. There are certain habits that separate the successful people from the less than successful group. The successful group is extremely organized and efficient, which is exactly how they get things done. But knowing that we all have the same 24-hours in a day, how does this successful, organized group get more done in a day than everyone else?

What Organized People Do That You Don't

The organized ones are the people who accomplish more in a day than the rest do. They are the ones who seem to have it all together. The ones who smash through one task after the next until they finally accomplish all that they set out to do, and they do this *while* making them for themselves, their hobbies, their passions, their family, and their friendships. *How do they do it all?* Well, it isn't a superpower; it's the little habits that they have that keep them organized and focused on what they should be doing that makes the difference. These are the habits that organized people live by, and if you're not already doing them, you should because it's going to lead to much better work-life balance *without* compromising on your responsibilities:

Avoid Relying Too Much on Your Brain to Store Information

Memory is fallible. Things fade, especially when you don't use them. Successful and organized people understand this, and that's why they choose to store information in a system that they trust. Now, what exactly separates a system that you can trust from one that you can't? Or one that is probably going to fail you? First and foremost, a system that you can trust is one that is not going to lose your data. This immediately rules out your brain because our brains forget things all the time. It may also rule out a paper notebook if you don't keep that notebook backed up in some other digital way. Apps like Evernote or OneNote or Google Drive or anything else that has redundant servers across the world will ensure your data is always backed up, even if the computer where you originally recorded that data. That system needs to be easily accessible, so make sure it's a cloud-accessible note-taking system.

Always Have A Backup

Anything that you use on a regular basis should have a backup. Running out of the things you need right in the middle of your work is going to hamper your productivity and concentration. Organized people always have a backup of the essential items they need to stay productive so that if they ever run out, they've always got a spare on hand that is ready to use. A quick rule of thumb to remember is this: *If running out something is going to cause an interruption in your life, always have a backup.*

Find A System That Works for You

Not your colleague, not your friend, not a relative, but for *you.* The reason you find it difficult sometimes to plow through a task is that the current system which you have is probably not working well for you. If that is the case, then it's time to copy what organized people do and create your own work system which works for you. Find a way or a system which makes you feel more motivated, and mold it to your current work habits. If tackling the most challenging tasks first is what works better for you, go ahead and do that.

Label All Things

Organized people are diligent about this too, especially with things they aren't' going to interact with for a long time. If you don't label it, you run the risk of forgetting all about it and what it's used for. Labeling your things makes it easy to remember exactly what each item is used for and this is going to save you a lot of time trying to figure it out again.

How to Maintain Better Work-Life Balance

The idea that we should continuously keep track of how much work we're putting in *and* to make sure we're still making time for the things we enjoy aside from our jobs seems like a massive challenge these days. Go back several decades ago before technology made it difficult to leave the office mentally even though you've done it physically, there was a clear distinction between work life and personal life. Before the internet, people used to clock in and out of work and once they left, they couldn't bring their work home with them anyway. The internet may have bridged billions of people around the world together, but it has also made it hard to separate ourselves from our work.

It is all about work-life balance, that is how people maintain our happiness and our motivation. It's important to take care of yourself, even when you're putting your 100% effort into a goal that you're doing. Doing too much too soon could lead to burning out quickly, especially when you don't enjoy the work that you're doing and associate it with negative emotions. Life can feel like a massive game of Jenga where you keep piling on your tasks and responsibilities on top of an already precariously tall pile, hoping that it's not going to fall over. Fatigue increase in stress levels, increased expectations on your employer's part, and a reduction in time spent on yourself and with your family and friends are just some of the negative consequences that happen when you don't prioritize work-life balance. This kind of lifestyle can never be sustained for long and it will eventually rob you of your happiness and motivation to do anything.

Start implementing to following strategies to achieve better work-life balance the way successful and organized people do and minimize the stress and unhappiness that you feel:

Define What Work-life Balance Looks Like to You

How much time do you need to allocate to both your work and personal life to feel happy and accomplished in both these areas? How much time do you need to allocate at work to ensure all your duties are met? What does winding-down time look like to you? Once you've determined what a balanced life looks like to you, start implementing the little steps you need to bring about the changes you want to see. For example, cut down the distraction time at work so you can squeeze more tasks in. Make it a point to ignore all work-related items once you've left the office at the end of the day. This may require having to talk to your supervisor and insist that they avoid calling you during the weekend and learning to say "no" more often, but if you balance this out by maximizing your productivity during your designated work hours, there shouldn't be a problem.

Don't Take Your Work Home with You

It really is that simple. Break the habit of bringing work home with you; there's no reason for you to feel guilty if you don't do it. You've already put in a good 7 to 8 hours of your time during the day to commit to your job; now it's time to take the rest of the day to commit to yourself. Leave your work where it belongs: *At the office*.

Turn Off Your Emails After Work Hours

Avoid bringing your work home with you. You've put in the hours that you needed at the office. Once you've clocked out, that's your "me" time and you should honor it by switching off your email notifications and making it a habit not to respond to anything else that comes up outside your work hours. This simple act of turning off your email notifications is such an easy way to minimize the stress that you feel and to ensure that you really enjoy the time that you should now be spending on yourself.

Increasing the Quality of Your Downtime

When you're taking time out for yourself, maximize the quality of your "me" time with self-care. Exercising, meditating, and yoga are examples of activities that help to reduce the stress you feel and they make you feel good when you're done. Getting the rest you need, spending time surrounding yourself with the love and companionship of family and friends are all ways to boost the happiness you feel when it's "me" time. The more you look after yourself, the happier you'll feel and when you do, your motivation is going to increase exponentially simply because you feel happier.

Chapter 4: Step 4 – Build Self-Discipline

Self-discipline. The ability to force yourself to do things that are congruent with your goals but may not necessarily be the things desires at the moment. Doing this through sheer willpower and determination is hard work and that's why it takes focus to really buckle down and stay consistent with what you're supposed to be doing. There's an interesting thought about self-discipline that comes from the Roman Emperor, Marcus Aurelius. Famously referred to as the last good emperor, Marcus Aurelius was also the most powerful man on earth at that time. He reflected every evening on the events of the day and wrote down his thoughts and observations in his diary, which would go on to be published as '*Meditations.*' It would become one of the most important, profound and significant sources of Stoic Philosophy.

In his *Meditations* book, there is a passage that has a lot to do with self-discipline. You might even say it could be considered the foundation of self-discipline. Aurelius writes this about self-discipline: "*At dawn, when you have trouble getting out of bed, tell yourself I have to go to work as a human being. What do I have to complain about if I am going to do the work I was born to do, the things I was brought into the world to do.*" A person who has self-discipline or restraint is not someone who does not feel any kind of desire. They do but they overcome their desires and cravings and abstain from things that will bring them negativity.

Why Do I Need Self-Discipline?

Because this is the driving force that is going to keep you motivated and not venture off the path to success. Because it'll help you be a better person all around. There is a very good reason why many of the most successful people in the world attribute their success to self-discipline. That's because it is an important skill that everyone should possess. It isn't something that is meant to strip you of any joy by forcing you to live a more restrictive and guided life than you would like. It is meant to help you stay on track to achieving your goals and reaching your full potential.

Without that extra push, that necessary kick in the butt, many of us would be guilty of slacking off far too much and taking things easy. After all, who would voluntarily opt to spend long hours working hard or sacrificing the things that they want to do, if they were given the option to do otherwise? If successful people can be driven by the actions that are demanded by their goals, there's no reason why you can't do the same. You need to focus on the path you have chosen and let that be strong enough to override your current desire. History is proof that when mankind wants something bad enough, nothing can stand in their way. They could be faced with a hundred obstacles and still persevere because they were driven, determined, and disciplined enough to see it through. Everyone could benefit from having some self-discipline instilled into their lives. It teaches you to stay focused. Those who have achieved success have done so because they remain focused on their goals, and self-discipline will not let them stray from that path until they have achieved what they want. It takes sheer, intense focus to remain on track.

Why Do So Many People Fail to Stay Disciplined?

Two words: *Instant gratification.* Yes, it is one of life's biggest enemies, and it is the reason that we fall off the wagon on the course to achieving success. The thought of having access to immediate pleasure now, instead of sacrificing and waiting for that pleasure to present itself in the future, is a thought that not many are able to resist and resisting it wouldn't be possible if we didn't have the self-discipline needed to help us along the way.

There's another enemy that strips you of self-discipline too. *Laziness.* Laziness is an enemy of productivity and self-discipline. Moreover, the pull and allure of laziness are so strong that succumbing to it is frighteningly easy. The minute you get sucked into the cycle of laziness, getting out can be very difficult. It certainly does not help that laziness is often accompanied by procrastination. Combining these two qualities often leads to disaster. They are the deadliest habits any person could have, and are usually the very reasons why you are not succeeding. Like an invisible force that is pulling you to the dark side, laziness is an enemy that you will often battle on your mission to become a more self-disciplined individual.

Key Steps to Building the Discipline You Need

The first thing you need to do is figure out your *"why"*? Why did you choose the goals that you did? What's the reason behind the actions you now decide to take? When you decided to go through this guide, what was your reason "why"? There is no easy way or shortcut towards gaining more self-discipline. You are going to have to put in the time, effort, and energy into the entire process if you want to make it happen. To become a disciplined person that you want to be to make the positive changes in your life that you hope to see, it is going to require some sacrifices on your part. Adjustments need to be made, and there are going to be some difficult things you might have to do, but change is necessary for the greater good, and this must be a sacrifice you must be willing to make.

Focus on the Change, Not the Goal

If focusing on the final goal is proving more of a challenge than you thought, create a shift in your mindset by focusing on the *change* that you want to see happen instead. Embrace the change that you want to see and you will find yourself acting in alignment with that change. Embrace the little changes that you want to see happen along the way and focus on that. Instead of focusing on the goal to lose 10 pounds, focus on the little changes you need to make each day, the changes that you can see right now. Like making healthier meal choices, exercising for 30-minutes today. Focus on the little steps makes it easier to find the discipline you need to carry out those actions *today* rather than focus on the far-away goal that needs time to work toward.

Change Your Immediate Environment

Achieving success is about taking control of not just your self-discipline, but of the environment where you spend a lot of your time. While external environments are not a big percentage that contributes to your success, they do make a difference in one way. An easy way to grasp this concept would be to imagine yourself in your office. Now picture it being neat, organized, with everything in its place, perfect ambiance, and lighting, just the right kind of environment which fuels you to be productive. Now, imagine your office space being messy, cluttered, papers and mess everywhere. How does that make you feel? It is easy to see how the former is a situation that is going to encourage productivity, while the latter is simply going to demotivate you from wanting to do anything, which is not going to help your self-discipline.

Frequent Reminders

We all could use a reminder every now and then, even more so when you're trying to cultivate the discipline you need. Whenever you struggle to take the steps you need, remind yourself why you decided to do this in the first place and why you need to be more disciplined. This is much easier to do once you've defined your "why." At the end of the day, you still need to have a strong enough reason for your actions if you want to do them consistently.

Learning to Embrace the Discomfort

Nothing that is worth having is ever going to come easy or be handed to you on a silver platter. Learning to embrace the discomfort as part of the journey is how you stay motivated and disciplined enough to keep putting on foot in front of the other. Each time you embrace discomfort, you're working on building and strengthening that self-discipline mental muscle. The key to winning at persistence is to focus on the solution, not the problem. You have to realize that setbacks, however difficult, are ultimately temporary. Thus, always see discomfort as an opportunity to work on building your self-discipline because that uncomfortable moment is not going to last forever.

Develop an Optimistic Outlook

Having an optimistic outlook is the first and most important key to developing persistence. It's the unwavering belief that no matter what happens, things will work out in the end. You can develop optimism by building and also improving your self-belief and self-confidence. Persistent and disciplined people do not just sit on their laurels, feeling sorry for themselves whenever challenges arise.

It's going to take some getting used to, and the initial adjustment could be difficult for many if you're not used to being disciplined with your routine, decisions, and actions. It's going to feel weird in the beginning, and there'll probably be several times when you're tempted to give into the urge to just quit, but don't. Don't do it. If you can push through the initial difficult phase during the beginning of the process, it will all be worth it and it only gets better from there. Soon, these habits will become so much a part of your routine that you don't even feel it anymore and it comes naturally to you without a second thought.

Chapter 5: Step 5 – Boost Your Productivity by Getting Things Done Faster

There's a very real problem with the world we live in today. The problem is our society is so focused on the concept of "more" that we take on unnecessary things we don't need, which ends up cluttering our lives and eventually making a mess that leads to lower levels of productivity and eventually kills self-motivation because we're so burned out from being stretched too thin. Today's society is battling an unholy alliance between three dominant forces, which are being addicted to technology like our smartphones, social media, and consumerism. While these are not necessarily all bad, there are some downsides to this fast-paced world that we're living in today, one of it is that society is now focused on the undisciplined pursuit of trying to bite off more than they can chew.

To become more self-motivated, you must protect your desire for greater productivity by protecting the greatest asset that you have at your disposal. *Time.* Your energy levels are going to decrease as you progress throughout your day, and thus, you need to save your creativity and the greatest energy levels for only the essential tasks and opportunities. You're going to have to be comfortable with letting all the other opportunities pass you by.

Boosting Productivity Levels

Increasing productivity begins with organizing your time better, and while the management skills here are going to help you get started in finding a system that works for you, remember to pick the methods which are going to be essential to your productivity.

Use the Deadline Method

Setting realistic deadlines increases your motivation to see it through. When you have fewer deadlines competing for your time and attention, you're less stressed about rushing to meet them all. In fact, with fewer commitments on your hands, you're able to set your own deadlines now based on how quickly you think you can work through and complete a task.

Schedule Your Tasks

Instead of trying to do 10 things in a day, you've trimmed it down to only 5 important tasks that you thought were essential to complete. With the 5 tasks that you have, you now need to learn how to schedule what needs to be attended to first based on priority and urgency. A to-do list is going to be very useful in this case, where you can list down all the 5 times you need to finish, organizing them in order of priority, and schedule how much time should be allocated towards each task.

Deliberate Choose to Set A Good Example

A surprisingly effective trick to boost productivity is to be a good example yourself. When you know that other people are watching you, especially if you happen to lead a team of people, you're not going to rest and take it easy. When you know that other people are holding you accountable for the success of the team, you're motivated to kick your productivity levels up a notch and get things done.

Aim to Wake Up Earlier

Successful people *love* waking up early and getting right to work. It is the one thing all of them have in common, starting their day as early as possible so they can get the most out of their day. Early risers have a few extra minutes in their day to think and plan how best to use their time. They also know that waking up early is the best way to optimize performance since energy levels tend to dip as the day progresses, which then affects productivity. Therefore, by waking up early, they tackle the most important tasks on their lists with energy and gusto, while the less important tasks are reserved for the end of the day when not so much energy is demanded of them.

Avoid Multitasking

Multitasking only gives the illusion of being more productive. Not only do successful people trim down the workload so they can manage their time better, but they also do it so they can avoid multitasking too. Multitasking may seem like an efficient approach to get more done in the same amount of time, but the truth is, it's not as efficient as you might think. In reality, multitasking is, in fact, hampering your productivity. When you're able to concentrate on one thing at a time, you're more focused. You're able to give 100% attention to one thing that you're doing, instead of giving only 50% attention to one task, and 50% attention on another.

Always Assume You Can Improve

Elon Musk once said: *"It's important to have a feedback loop where you're constantly thinking about what you've done and what you can do to make it better."* No matter how proud he may be of his accomplishments and what his company has been able to achieve, Musk is never satisfied with where he is right now. He knows there is always a better and faster way of doing things, and adopting this same approach is how you improve your productivity levels too. What could you be doing better? What could you be doing more efficiently that is going to save you time without compromising quality? How do you improve on your system so you spend less time on your tasks and not sacrifice your work-life balance? Your potential is only limited by your willingness to work until you find an effective solution and knowing that there are better ways of getting things done is what you need to keep you motivated and productive.

The Gamification Technique

Have you heard the term *"Gamification"*? It is a technique where a person takes the mechanics of gaming and infuses that with different areas of their life to fuel their motivation. You see, when something is fun and enjoyable, we're a lot more likely to willingly participate in it. More than that, we're *engaged* in what we're doing because we're having fun while we do it. But before that, here's an important point to take note of: *Just because something is fun does not mean it is motivating, and just because something is motivating does not mean that it is fun.* For example, you might be motivated to do push-ups, but that doesn't mean it is fun to do. Working on your project is something you enjoy, but you might not feel motivated to do it. Sometimes you *don't want to do something*, even though you know that once you get into it, you'll enjoy it. Fun and motivation are *not the same things* and they do not automatically come in a package.

There is a connection between the two, and that connection is *gamification*. Any facet of your life can be spruced up through gamification, and if you're struggling with finding the "fun" in the activities you dislike doing, this could be the solution you've been searching for. When you're playing a game, you're motivated by the rewards that you collect throughout the different levels you're progressing through. Behaviorally we skew towards making decisions that give us the most immediate benefit or reward. This is especially true if the consequences are in the distant future and why instant gratification can be so hard to ignore.

Our brain is a highly skilled reward detector. Ours is a brain that is addicted has learned to prioritize and seek reward ahead of anything else. There's something so rewarding about progressing through the different stages of a game. Seeing those notifications pop up that let you know you've succeeded and you're moving on to the next level keeps you addicted to the game and coming back for more. If notifications could pop up like that in real life each time we accomplished a small feat, we would probably enjoy the tasks we had to do a lot more. Games have a very clear goal and progression system, and if you apply those same principles in everyday life, your motivation is going to skyrocket, fueled by that desire to level up, so to speak.

Gamification takes mundane tasks and adds an element of fun into it, which then motivates you to keep going because you're enjoying the process. We all need to find what motivates us to keep us going, and there's nothing wrong with allowing little rewards for yourself whenever you've finished a job if that is what you need to keep you moving. Gamification is a completely personal process, and you could make it as interesting or exciting as you wanted. You could even assign points to tasks depending on the level of complexity, the same way it works within the dynamics of a game. The tasks that take longer earn more points and the easier tasks earn fewer points. You would then assign a reward based on the different point tiers.

If having little rewards to look forward to at the end of the task keeps you going, tell yourself before you begin each task that you're going to finish this task per the deadline you set for yourself and enjoy your much-needed reward at the end. The reward could be anything you like, a favorite meal, watching an episode or two of your favorite TV shows, perhaps a few minutes spent browsing social media, anything that will make you look forward to it and keep you motivated to do the things that need to be done. Just like a game, the more levels you progress through or the more tasks you get done in the day, the greater the reward at the end and this time, you won't feel so guilty about indulging because you know that you've earned it.

Chapter 6: Step 6 – Tap into the Power of Reading

In a world where entertainment is literally in the palm of your hands now, you may be asking yourself *what is the point of reading?* Ever since the days of the earliest humans and for as long as we can remember, people have always had a thirst for gathering information. We do it naturally from a very young age. We learn to talk, read, and communicate through various mediums to transmit and receive information constantly. As time went by and life started moving faster and faster, especially with the introduction of technology, it's only natural that we start trying to do things faster too. Like reading at a much quicker pace, since the faster we move, the more information we absorb. The faster we move; the quicker things get done.

Why Do We Need to Read?

In today's fast-paced world, reading is becoming a dying habit because there are much faster ways to consume information. If you're not reading a lot, you're missing out on a lot and you'll find it much harder to achieve the success you want. Why? Well, here are the surprising benefits of reading that you might not have thought about:

It's Food for Your Brain

Our bodies need food to sustain itself and function optimally, and so does the brain. Our brain needs to continuously learn to function at peak performance. The best part is reading both fiction and non-fiction can give you the same benefit. Reading has the power to change your brain structure and improve your cognitive processes.

It Improves Your Focus and Concentration

Have you ever felt your mind start to drift in the middle of reading a piece of content that wasn't particularly interesting? You don't enjoy reading it, but you have to, and you struggle to retain the focus and concentration needed to plow through the material. Daydreaming and a lack of focus is another common problem faced by many readers, even more so when the pings and beeps of our mobile devices easily shift our attention away from what we're supposed to be doing. Reading regularly helps to train you to stay focused and pay attention to the material that you're reading. Train yourself often enough with enjoyable fiction and you'll soon be able to apply this same level of concentration even with non-fictional dry material.

Your Knowledge Improves

The more you read, the smarter you become. By consistently consuming information, you keep your brain functioning in peak performance. Being knowledgeable on a wide range of subjects improves confidence and self-esteem, and you'll be more motivated to seize opportunities when you believe you have the skills and now the knowledge to do so.

You Communicate Better

Books are fantastic tools that help you expand your vocabulary, which you can then use to express yourself better. Your speech becomes refined and intelligent and you become more empowered to participate in interesting and beneficial conversations with intelligent people. You are the average of the five people you surround yourself with, and when you surround yourself with successful and intelligent people, you eventually become just like them too.

It's A Cheaper Way to Gain A Mentor

When you read a book written by someone who has already achieved success, it's almost like you're being mentored directly by them. Think about how much a successful person's knowledge is worth. People are willing to pay thousands of dollars to have lunch with Warren Buffet but since not everyone has that kind of money, books are just as good of a mentor. The book is the words, ideas, the mindset, advice, and experience that the successful person has to share and they have compiled all the information they know into a book. It's almost as if they are speaking directly to you. The knowledge that you get from reading is irreplaceable.

It Expands Your Horizons

Reading encourages you to keep an open mind. When you read, you interact with different people, different stories, different materials and ideas, a lot of which could be very different from your own. This helps to open your mind and be more accepting of others. A mind that is opened is a mind that judges less and is more accepting of people and the world around them. An open mind is the kind of mindset needed to build the foundation of success.

Tips to Boost Your Reading Habit

The following strategies will help you develop your reading habit until you eventually become a more consistent reader:

Have A Page Goal

Set a certain number of pages that you will aim to read daily and turn that into a habit. This is another habit productive people do, and this is an exercise anyone can start doing right away. Get out of bed each morning with a purpose. Tell yourself, *"Today, I have to accomplish..."* In the case of improving your reading habits, your daily goal could be *"Today, I will finish that 10 pages of reading."* Even if the goal or the task at hand may be something small, training yourself to wake up each day with a purpose and intention to get things done is what helps train them to get into the productive mindset and way of thinking.

Read in The Morning

Read while you're having your morning cup of coffee or on your commute to work. Making it a habit to read first thing in the morning is the best way to make sure that you never miss a day. As the day progresses, you day fills up with the tasks you're supposed to be doing, your energy levels drop progressively, and by the time you've reached the end of the day, you're no longer motivated to read because you're too tired.

Read After You Exercise

As your body takes the time to cool down before you hit the shower, take this time to squeeze in reading a couple of pages. Exercise primes your brain for learning, balancing the neurotransmitters in your brain, which, in turn, improve your ability to pay attention and prime your brain to efficiently absorb and remember new information.

Make the Process Enjoyable

The gamification method could prove useful here. Go to the coffee shop, get a cup of coffee, sit down in a comfortable chair, and make the reading process much more enjoyable. If you've got a comfortable spot in your home that does the trick, you can do it right in the comfort of your own home too. The more you enjoy the process, the less likely you are to find reasons not to do it, and with the gamification method in play, having those little rewards to look forward to at the end of your tasks makes picking up a book and reading even more enjoyable.

Get Rid of Distractions

Avoiding distractions is an absolute must if you're going to focus on the content you're reading. You want a space that is quiet and comfortable, where you can easily settle into as you start working on your concentration levels. It is very important that you remain comfortable throughout the session because if you aren't, you're going to become easily distracted and bothered by the levels of discomfort that you feel, which will then make it hard for you to even get started off on the right foot with your new reading habit. Distraction-free zones are a good habit to start adopting if you haven't already done it before.

Make Reading Part of Your Routine

The most driven and successful individuals in this world have a which they stick to religiously. That's because a good routine can set the tone for how your day goes. This applies when you're trying to cultivate better reading habits too. Part of sticking to the techniques you're trying to learn is to remain motivated to do so. A good reading habit routine would be to feel excited each time you're about to read something, regardless of what it is. Dwindling motivation is a common problem when the material that you're about to read is dry, so try to get into the habit of making it a routine to feel excited and enthusiastic each time you need to read (the gamification technique would work really well here again). Remember, every material is teaching you something new.

Be Accountable

Making yourself accountable to someone else is a great way to keep you on track with your reading habit. Enlist the help of a friend or family member and tell them if you do not read at least 20-pages a day every single day for the next 3-months, you would have to pay them $100 dollars. When skipping out on days is quite literally going to cost you money, it's not going to be as tempting to skip out on them anymore. Track your progress every day on a spreadsheet is another way of holding yourself accountable and the visual element of seeing your steady progress has the added benefit of serving as a motivational factor. The accountability factor and actually telling other people about your progress is a lot more motivating than keeping it to yourself.

Chapter 7: Step 7 – Declutter Your Environment

A space and mind that is chaotic and filled with clutter is not an environment where motivation can thrive. Clutter is a distraction, and building an environment that facilitates focus means you're going to need to declutter your environment fast. Physical possessions are more than just the stuff that surrounds your external environment. They are a manifestation of what is going on inside your mind. Your phone bills. Your laundry. Your cabinets and shelves full of unused items, stuff you may have even forgotten that you own. The couches and chairs piled with old papers, books, and magazines in the corner gathering dust. The unnecessary, non-essential items in your life that take up so much room and space that they start to feel like a burden that is weighing down.

Do you feel like you can relate? The good news is, the stuff you have now and your past *does not* define who you are. Each new day is an opportunity to live better and more intentionally than you did the day before and it starts with renewing your motivation once more through a process called *decluttering*.

What Are Decluttering and Minimalism?

A lot of the items that we own are, truth be told, not essential. You don't need the same shirt in multiple colors. You don't need 10 pairs of jeans when you keep wearing the only two because you like those best. You don't need several books lined up on the bookshelves if you have no interest in ever reading them again. Most people are drowning in their own clutter and they don't even know it. Our inability to organize our thoughts in our head is manifesting external, and if you stop to take a good look at what your immediate environment looks like, ask yourself this one question: *Do I really need all these items?*

Joshua Fields Millburn and Ryan Nicodemus, authors of *Minimalism: Live a Meaningful Life* defined minimalism as "a tool to rid yourself of life's excess for focusing on what's important, so you can find happiness, fulfillment, and freedom." Nobody ever wants to be unhappy, and while we know that we need to work on happiness internally, we also need to work on it externally, which means creating an environment around us that helps us focus on what's important in our lives. You *own* your possessions, not the other way around. It doesn't matter where you are at or what other people think, and it doesn't matter how fast or how slow you declutter. It doesn't matter if you want to live your life with more simplicity or become a minimalist.

The journey to declutter your life is going to be messy at times. It can feel unpleasant and it can feel hard to keep going. But it's all going to feel so worthwhile once you feel your motivation and willpower coming back when you're no longer distracted by the unnecessary clutter in your life. With a clear purpose in your life and without the unnecessary distractions taking away your focus, you will once more be able to see your purpose and what you want to accomplish in your life. Nothing is going to feel better than a life of simplicity and peace.

Declutter Your Life for Good

The first thing you need to do is break your life down into categories. When you look at your life as a whole, there are several areas that could benefit from a little decluttering. However, trying to approach it as a whole is going to overwhelm you, especially when you've already got a lot of stuff going on as it is. When you once more begin to focus on yourself, it reminds you of what you have been neglecting all along. That you matter more than any material possessions you could possibly buy, and when you start to focus on yourself again, your mental and physical health starts to shine because you're working on becoming a better you. Let's look at some of these categories right now and how to declutter your life for good:

Declutter Your Home

This is the easiest place to start. Aside from work, your home is where you spend most of your time in. Your material possessions, everything that you own and have in your home right now, is taking up a lot more of your time than you realize. How much time do you spend cleaning up your home? How much time do you spend arranging and rearranging stuff around your home or your office workspace whenever you feel things are getting too messy? The more you own, the more time you end up wasting on doing unnecessary cleaning and clearing. Valuable time that could instead be spent on working towards achieving your goals, or doing something to better yourself. All the material possessions demand a lot more of our time to upkeep then we realize. Do you want to make the most of your time more productively? Start by decluttering your home environment.

Declutter Your Paperwork

It is easier than ever to go paperless and that is what you should opt to do. Going paperless isn't even going to be completely difficult because everything you need can be stored either on your mobile or on a cloud drive for easy access anytime, anywhere. You're saving the trees, doing good for the environment, and reducing the amount of paper clutter in your home. Only keep the documents that are vital, like your birth certificate, for example, contracts and agreements where you genuinely need to have a hard copy around. Otherwise, put it on the cloud and go paperless.

Declutter Your Workspace

Whether at home or in the office, an uncluttered workspace is a beautiful thing to look at. Those beautiful pictures online just inspire you to sit down and work for hours because of how peaceful it looks, with the bright sunlight streaming through the windows and nothing but a laptop and a coffee mug on your desk. Which makes you reflect on what your current workspace looks like right now. Keep it neat, clean, and clutter-free except for one of two items. Unless you're actively working on some papers or documents, there should be none of these on your desk at any time. Post-it notes should be tucked away in your drawers until you need them, along with any pens, stapler, or other basic stationery which you use regularly. Anything that is unnecessary and not contributing to your work routine needs to go.

Declutter the People

A messy home and busy work environment is not the only culprit that tends to drain your energy; people do it too. You simply don't have enough time or energy on your hand to juggle both people that drain your energy and the unnecessary work in your day that take up more energy than it should. Energy management is going to call for decluttering. Declutter everything from your daily task list that is not a priority, and declutter the negative people in your life who do nothing more than make you feel exhausted each time you're in their company.

Declutter Your Digital Devices

Oh yes, even digital devices are not spared here. Computers, laptops, mobile phones, tablets, even smartwatches are supposedly here to simplify our lives and make things easier so we spend less time on our workload, but it has become quite the opposite. If the lifestyle that we lead is already naturally cluttered already, this tends to carry over onto our digital lives too. All the extra "hours" you supposedly would have gained from quicker and faster internet processes have now been lost wading through mountains of emails that need to be sorted out, searching for documents online, and of course, countless hours spent aimlessly browsing through social media apps. Decluttering begins with your social media apps, and it's time to work through them one by one. You don't need to delete your accounts, but you do need to start thinking about downsizing in terms of your connections and who you follow. Facebook friends that you barely know or haven't had a real conversation within years don't need to be on your list, delete them.

Productivity can be running low when you're distracted by all the mess that is surrounding you. Not just at home, but at work too. A messy cubicle and work desk can make it hard to get anything done, even more so if you spend far too much time looking for items because you can't find them among the mess. Being constantly stressed out tends to deplete you of your motivation. You may think you're not stressed or bothered too much by the piles of clutter you see around you, but subconsciously you are. The freedom that you get by living with less can be a lot more liberating than you may think. It's not just about downsizing all your belongings for the sake of clearing away the mess in your home alone. No, it is much more than that. It is about clearing your entire life and redefining it to have more purpose and meaning than it once did before. You will be amazed at how this experience can bring you a sense of peace, not just in your home, but in every other aspect of your life too.

Conclusion

Thank you for making it through to the end of *"How to Stay Motivated"*, let's hope it was informative and able to provide you with all of the tools you need to achieve your goals whatever they may be.

Motivation is an easy enough thing to reclaim once you know what you need to do. If your current routine isn't working for you, it's time to change things up. Sometimes, it's not about being unable to motivate yourself; rather, you're *unwilling to do it* because it feels too difficult. Your motivation and willingness to do something for the long-term benefit are in a constant battle with your impulses and immediate desires, not to mention the never-ending distractions that seem to fill our day and try to grab our attention, no matter how hard we try to ignore them.

The good news is, you now have all the tools and key information you need to start building a system or effective routine for yourself that will gradually enhance your motivation. In a perfect world, we would always be thinking about the big picture, the future outcome we want to achieve and that would be enough to motivate us to kick things into gear and start taking action. Unfortunately, we don't live in an ideal world. We live in the real world where our impulsive desires and distractions at the moment are often what rules our minds more than anything else. This is why you need to create systems that will help you overcome these challenges and keep your willpower, motivation, and determination to get things done going strong.

More by Miles Toole

Discover all books from the Personal Productivity Series by Miles Toole at:

bit.ly/miles-toole

Book 1: *How to Be Productive*

Book 2: *How to Manage Time*

Book 3: *How to Be Organized*

Book 4: *How to Stay Focused*

Book 5: *How to Set Goals*

Book 6: *How to Stop Procrastinating*

Book 7: *How to Change Habits*

Book 8: *How to Stay Motivated*

Themed book bundles available at discounted prices:

bit.ly/miles-toole